A to Z

OF ROCKS, MINERALS, AND GEMS

Quarto is the authority on a wide range of topics.

Quarto educates, entertains and enriches the lives of
our readers—enthusiasts and lovers of hands-on living.

www.quartoknows.com

Written by Claudia Evans
Design and editorial: Evolution Design & Digital Ltd (Kent)

This edition first published in 2020 by QED Publishing,
an imprint of The Quarto Group.
The Old Brewery, 6 Blundell Street,
London N7 9BH, United Kingdom.
T (0)20 7700 6700 F (0)20 7700 8066
www.QuartoKnows.com

ISBN 978-0-7112-5684-2

Manufactured in Guangdong, China CC042020

9 8 7 6 5 4 3 2 1

A TO Z

OF ROCKS, MINERALS, AND GEMS

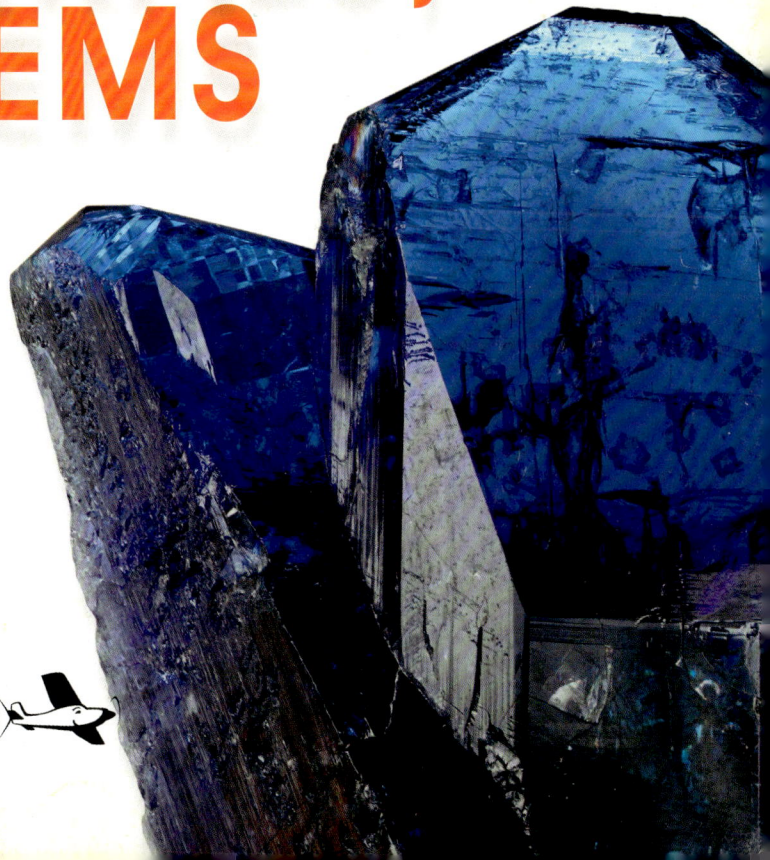

QED

CONTENTS

ROCKY PLANET

Wherever we are on Earth, there is **rock** beneath our feet. Sometimes we can see rock clearly, in cliffs and on mountains. Other times it is hidden beneath streets or grass. Rock forms mountains, creates waterfalls and can also contain beautiful and useful **minerals**.

Our Planet

At the centre of the Earth is a ball of super-hot **metal**, called the inner core. It is made mostly of iron and nickel. The inner core is surrounded by a layer of liquid metal called the outer core. The mantle is the next, and largest, layer and is made of rock, but it is so hot that the rock has melted in places. On top of the mantle is the crust, which forms the Earth's surface. The crust is made of cool, solid rock.

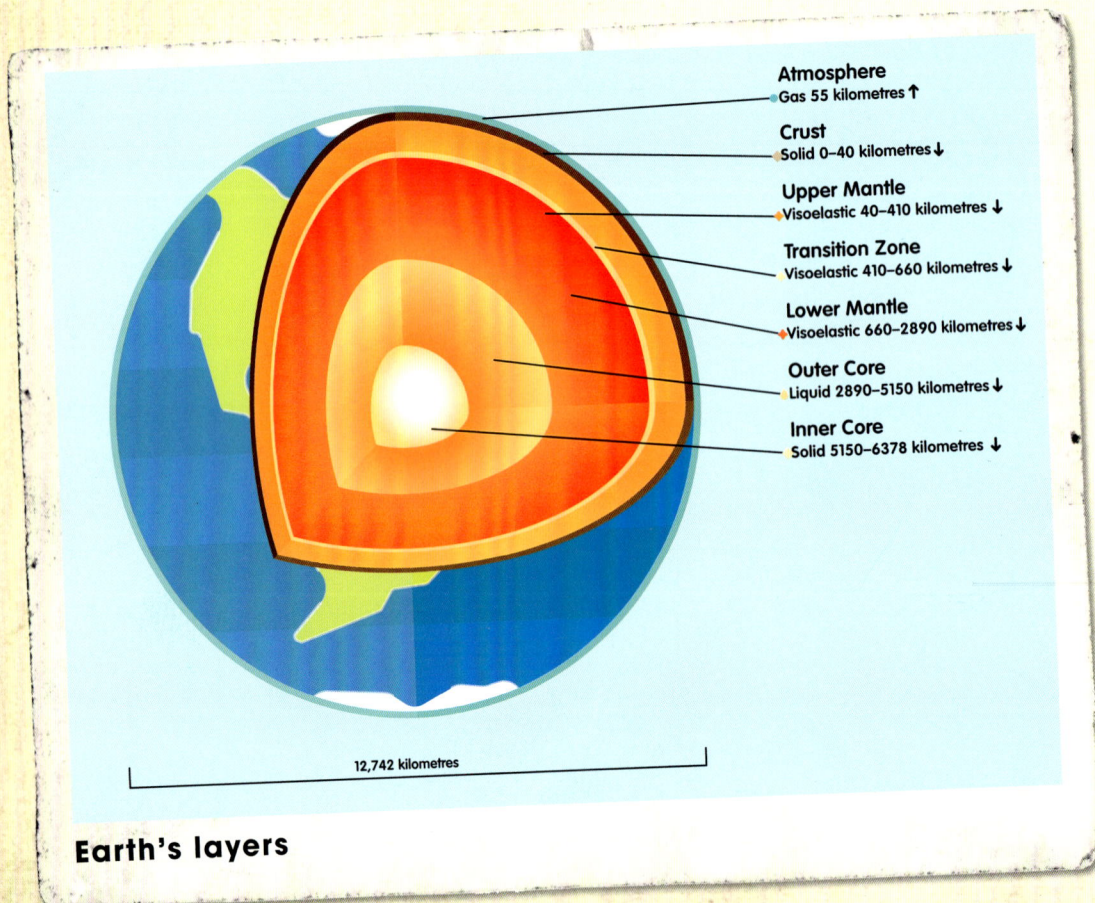

Atmosphere
Gas 55 kilometres ↑

Crust
Solid 0–40 kilometres ↓

Upper Mantle
Visoelastic 40–410 kilometres ↓

Transition Zone
Visoelastic 410–660 kilometres ↓

Lower Mantle
Visoelastic 660–2890 kilometres ↓

Outer Core
Liquid 2890–5150 kilometres ↓

Inner Core
Solid 5150–6378 kilometres ↓

12,742 kilometres

Earth's layers

Earth's Birth

Earth formed around 4.5 billion years ago, in a thick cloud of dust that was swirling around the Sun. At first, the Earth was so hot that even its surface was melted. After a few million years, the Earth cooled enough for its crust to become solid rock.

How to Use this Book

In this book, rocks and minerals are rated for their hardness on a scale of 1 to 10. This scale is called the Mohs scale, created by mineral collector Friedrich Mohs in 1812.

The Mohs scale measures a rock or mineral's hardness by how easily it can be scratched. Chalk is a very soft rock that can be scratched by a fingernail, so it is a 1 on the Mohs scale. Diamonds are very hard minerals that can only be scratched by other diamonds, so they are a 10 on the Mohs scale.

1-2: Very soft
3-4: Soft
5-6: Medium
7-8: Hard
9-10: Very hard

WHAT IS A MINERAL?

Minerals are solids that grow in the ground or in water. There are more than 5000 different types of minerals. Some minerals are useful, while others are considered pretty, so we search for them at the Earth's surface or by digging them out from mines.

Atoms

Like everything else on Earth, minerals are made of **atoms**. Atoms are so tiny that billions of them would fit on the head of a pin. When a material is made of only one type of atom, we call it an **element**. Iron and oxygen are two common elements found on Earth.

This helmet is made from the element iron.

Joining Together

Most minerals are made when different atoms stick together in a regular pattern. If a mineral continues to grow in this same pattern, it will form a **crystal** with a symmetrical shape.

Gems

If a mineral is pretty and difficult to break or scratch, it is often used in jewellery. These beautiful, hard minerals are called **gemstones**. When a gemstone is rare, it can be very expensive.

A spinel crystal has four sides, making a square.

Musgravite is a rare and expensive gemstone.

WHAT IS A ROCK?

A rock is made up of one or more minerals. Different mineral mixtures can make a rock hard or soft, dark or light, speckled or stripy.

Mineral Mix

Sometimes the mineral crystals in a rock are so small that we cannot see them. In other rocks the crystals have grown large, giving the rock spots. Sometimes the crystals have been pressed so they are lined up in rows, creating stripes.

In this pegmatite rock, the different colors of mineral crystals can be seen.

Useful Rocks

When a rock is strong, people cut it into slabs for use in construction. Rocks that are smooth and nicely coloured are carved into sculptures or jewellery. Some rocks are ground up to make gravel, then used as an ingredient in concrete.

Rock Types

People who study rocks are called **geologists**. They organize rocks into three groups, depending on how they were formed. These groups are igneous, sedimentary and metamorphic rocks.

These construction workers are making concrete, which will harden as it dries.

Geologists study rocks to figure out how they were made.

IGNEOUS ROCKS

Igneous rocks are made from rock that has melted inside the Earth. When the melted rock cools, it hardens into igneous rock.

Magma or Lava

When melted rock is underground, it is called magma. When magma spills out of a volcano, it is called lava. Igneous rocks are made of either magma or lava.

Lava

Magma

Made Inside

Sometimes magma cools and hardens while it is underground. This makes 'intrusive' igneous rock. This type of rock cools down slowly, allowing large mineral crystals to form.

Made Outside

When lava flows out of a volcano, it makes 'extrusive' igneous rock. This type of rock cools quickly in the open air or in seawater. The rock's mineral crystals are small because the rock cools before they have time to grow large.

Peridotite is formed inside the Earth.

Dacite is made of lava that erupted from a volcano.

SEDIMENTARY ROCKS

Sedimentary rocks are made from **sediment**, which is little bits of rocks, minerals or dead plants and animals. Over thousands or even millions of years, the sediment is **compressed**, which means it is pressed together with great force, and hardens into rock.

Bits of Rock

Sedimentary rocks are often made from bits of rock that have been broken off by waves, wind or rivers. The pebbles, sand or mud are carried along by rivers or waves until they pile up on the floor of a lake or ocean. When the sediment is buried and pressed under more sediment, it slowly hardens.

Shale is made from hardened mud.

Bits of Living Things

Some sedimentary rocks are made from sea creatures that died millions of years ago. When their shells and skeletons piled up on the seafloor, they were compressed until they hardened. Dead plants can also turn into rock if they collect at the bottom of a swamp or lake.

Chert is made from the bodies of tiny sea creatures called diatoms.

Bits of Mineral

Sometimes sedimentary rocks form in water that is full of floating bits of minerals. This type of rock can grow quickly if the water starts to **evaporate**. As the water disappears, the solid mineral bits are left behind and create sedimentary rocks.

METAMORPHIC ROCKS

Metamorphic rocks are made when any type of rock is changed by pressure or heat. The look and feel of the new rock depends on what rock it was made from and how it was formed.

Heated by Magma

When hot magma is close to solid rock, it can bake the rock with its heat. The closer a rock is to the magma, the harder it will be baked.

This hard basalt rock was baked by the heat of magma.

Pressed and Folded

Rocks can be squeezed and folded by movements in the Earth's crust. When the mineral crystals in a rock are pressed hard, they line up with each other, making layered rocks.

Schist is made when mudstone is pressed hard by movements in the Earth's crust.

A

AGATE

Type: Mineral

Colour: Multicoloured

Hardness: 6.5–7

Agate usually forms inside holes in old, hardened lava. It grows in layers, making bands of different colours. It is often made into jewellery or statues.

ALEXANDRITE

Type: Mineral

Colour: Appears to change

Hardness: 8.5

Alexandrite is a rare and expensive gem. It is famous for seeming to change colour in different lights. When seen in daylight, it looks emerald green. In artificial light, it becomes red. This colour-changing effect is caused by the way the crystal soaks up light.

A

AMAZONITE

Type: Mineral

Colour: Green to turquoise

Hardness: 6–6.5

Amazonite was used as a gem in ancient Egypt, where it was prized for its bright colour. Today, this mineral is often mistaken for jade because of its blue-green colour. Amazonite usually grows in four-sided blocks inside holes and cracks in rock.

ANDESITE

Type: Igneous rock

Colour: Light to dark grey

Hardness: 7

Andesite is lava that has run down the sides of a volcano, then cooled and hardened quickly. The rock gets its name from the Andes Mountains in South America, where there are many steep-sided volcanoes that spew out andesite.

A

ANGLESITE

Type: Mineral

Colour: Colourless, white, grey or yellow

Hardness: 3–3.5

This mineral gets its name from the place where it was first found: the island of Anglesey, off the coast of Wales. Anglesite contains lead, a metal that makes this mineral heavy.

APATITE

Type: Mineral

Colour: Green, blue, yellow, pink or brown

Hardness: 5

Apatite contains phosphorus, which helps plants to grow when it is in the soil. Apatite is often dug from the ground in mines, then turned into **fertilizer**, which is spread over soil.

ARAGONITE

Type: Mineral

Colour: Usually colourless to white or grey

Hardness: 3.5-4

Aragonite can grow in water that contains calcium carbonate. As the water evaporates, specks of calcium carbonate are left behind. They stick together, slowly making crystals of aragonite.

A

ARCHES

If rocks are battered by weather, rivers or ocean waves, they can start to crumble. When rocks crumble and wear away, we call it **erosion**. Sometimes rocks are worn away into amazing shapes, like arches.

Sea Arches

At the seaside, cliffs are beaten by waves. An arch can form in a headland, where cliffs curve out into the sea. An arch is most likely to form where cliffs are made of a soft rock, like chalk. First, the powerful waves crack the rock. Over time the crack grows into a cave. Eventually, the cave grows so large that it goes right through the headland, forming an arch.

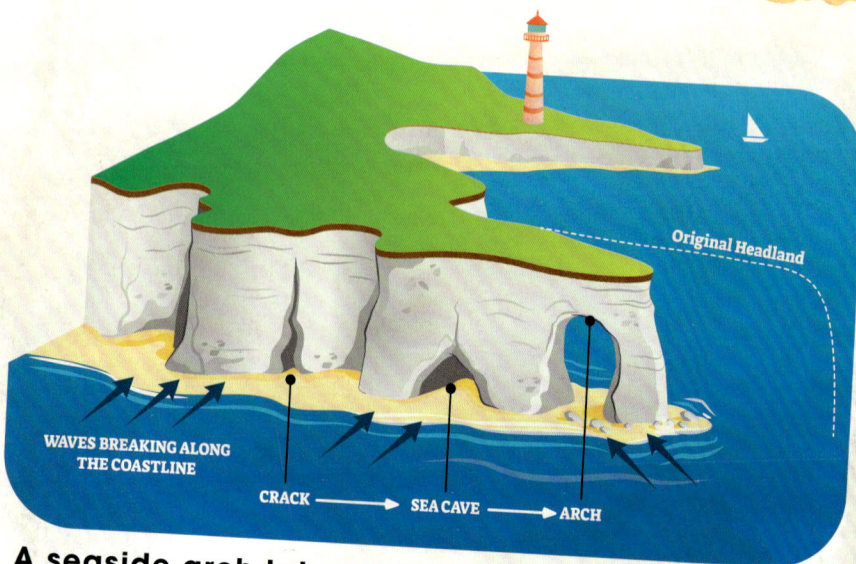

Original Headland

WAVES BREAKING ALONG
THE COASTLINE

CRACK ⟶ SEA CAVE ⟶ ARCH

A seaside arch takes thousands of years to form.

Land Arches

Far from the sea, arches can form in soft rocks such as sandstone. This is most likely to happen in a desert, where the rock is not covered by trees or grass. First, rainwater soaks into the rock. In the winter, that water freezes into ice, causing the rock around it to crumble. The wind then blows away the crumbly rock. Over millions of years, an arch slowly takes shape.

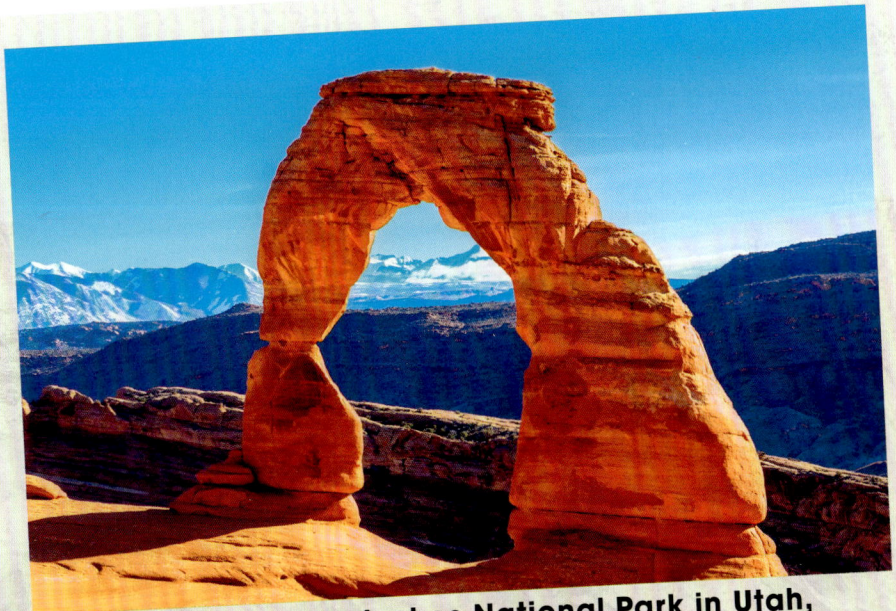

This arch is found in Arches National Park in Utah, United States.

B

BASALT

Type: Igneous rock

Colour: Grey to black, but turns rust red on the surface

Hardness: 6

Basalt is the most common igneous rock. It forms from runny, dark-coloured lava, which spreads over a large area before hardening. The Giant's Causeway in Northern Ireland is made of basalt that cracked into hexagonal pillars as it cooled.

B

BERYL

Type: Mineral

Colour: Colourless, green, blue, yellow or pink

Hardness: 7.5–8

This mineral is colourless, but as it grows it can be coloured by extra ingredients that get into the mix. Green beryl, coloured by the element chromium, is known as emerald, which is an expensive gem. Turquoise beryl is called aquamarine, while pink beryl is morganite.

BIOTITE

Type: Mineral

Colour: Usually brown to black, but may be yellow or white

Hardness: 2.5–3

Biotite is commonly found in igneous and metamorphic rocks. A thin sheet of biotite is bendy. This mineral is sometimes ground up and used in wall paints to improve the paint's texture. It stops the paint from cracking once it has dried.

BRECCIA

Type: Sedimentary rock

Colour: Mixed

Hardness: 7

Breccia is made when small chunks of rock are surrounded by sand or mud. This might happen at the bottom of a mountain or river. Over thousands of years, all that material hardens, forming breccia. The ancient Egyptians and Romans made buildings and sculptures from breccia.

CALCITE

Type: Mineral

Colour: Usually colourless or white, but may be grey, yellow or green

Hardness: 3

Calcite is made by many sea creatures to form their shells. Rocks made from crushed shells, such as limestone, contain lots of calcite. In limestone caves, crystals of calcite can grow where water with pieces of floating calcite has evaporated. Calcite can also grow into **stalactites** as water drips from the cave ceiling.

CASSITERITE

Type: Mineral

Colour: Black, brown, grey or green

Hardness: 6–7

This mineral contains the metal tin. Cassiterite is often mined for tin, which is often used for coating the cans used to hold food.

C

CAVES

A cave is a hole in rock that is big enough for people to explore. Some caves are many kilometres long and stretch deep underground.

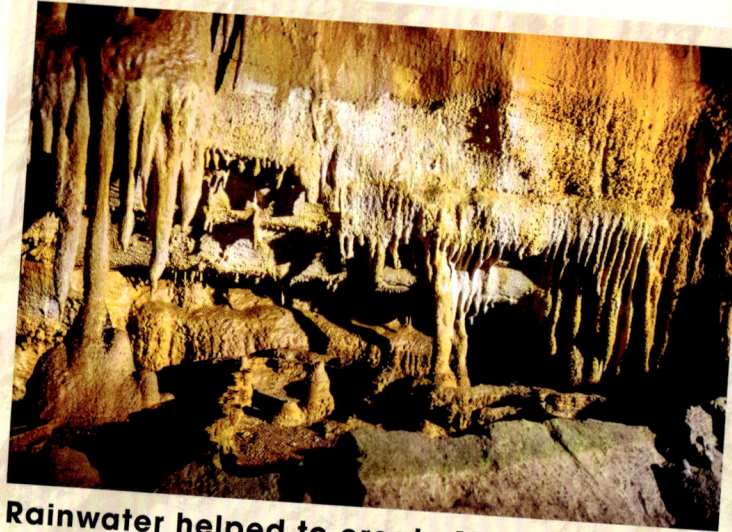

Rainwater helped to create Mammoth Cave in Kentucky, in the United States, which is the longest cave system in the world.

Made by Rainwater

Many caves are made by rainwater that has soaked into the ground. This water is slightly acidic, like vinegar. It can wear away rocks such as chalk, dolomite, limestone and marble to slowly create a cave.

Made by Waves

Waves can wear away cliffs to create seaside caves. Once the seawater is able to flow inside, the rock is worn away even faster, making the cave larger.

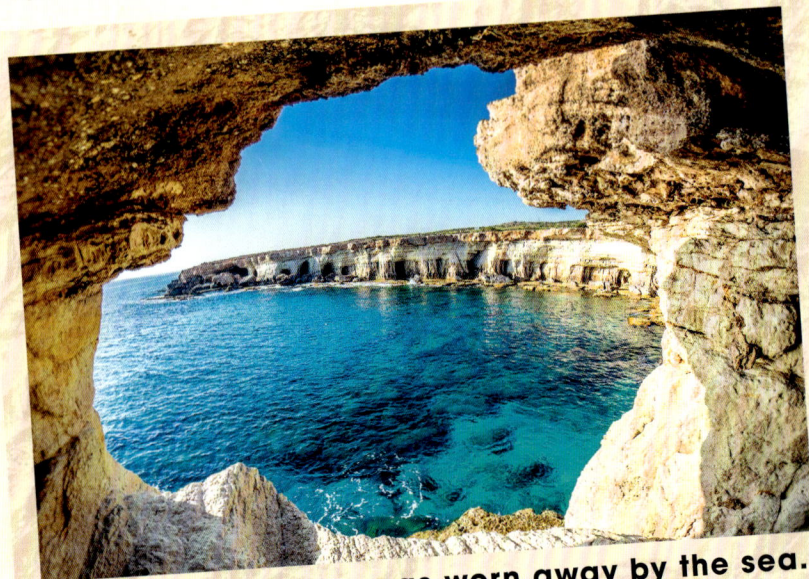

This cave in Cyprus was worn away by the sea.

Made by Wind

In deserts, strong wind blows sand against walls of rock. Over long periods of time, the sand can carve a cave into the rock face.

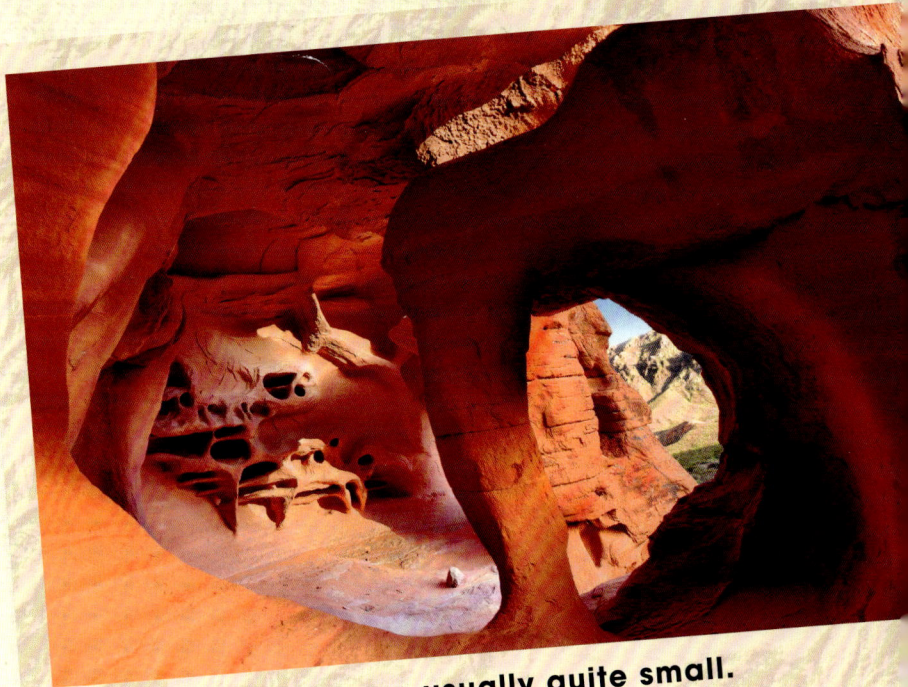

Wind-blown caves are usually quite small.

Made by Lava

As lava runs down the side of a volcano, its surface cools quickly into rock. Beneath the cool, hard surface, the hot lava continues to flow. Once the lava flow stops, it can leave behind a tube of rock.

Flowing lava created this cave in Hawaii.

33

C

CHALK

Type: Sedimentary rock

Colour: White

Hardness: 1

Chalk is made from the shells of tiny sea creatures such as coccoliths. These shells pile up on the seafloor, then are compressed until they harden into rock. Chalk is a very soft rock, so it is easily worn away into strange shapes by waves or wind.

COAL

Type: Sedimentary rock
Colour: Brown to black
Hardness: 1–1.5

It takes millions of years for coal to form. First, dead plants are trapped in a swamp. Then the plants are covered by layers of mud, which compresses them until they harden. Coal is dug from the ground because it is a fuel, giving off heat when it is burned. Burning coal also damages our **atmosphere**.

COPPER

Type: Metal

Colour: Pinkish orange

Hardness: 2.5-3

Metals can be found in the ground in big chunks or little flakes – or mixed in with other materials. Copper is a very useful metal because it is easy to bend and electricity flows through it. It is used in electrical wires.

DIAMOND

Type: Mineral

Colour: Usually colourless, but may be any colour

Hardness: 10

This super-strong mineral is made of just one element: carbon. Diamonds form deep inside the Earth. Pure diamonds are colourless and clear. They are often cut and polished until they sparkle, then used in jewellery.

DIORITE

Type: Igneous rock

Colour: Grey or black with paler speckles

Hardness: 7

This dark-speckled rock is formed from melted magma deep inside the Earth. It is not very common on Earth's surface, but it has been pushed to the surface in some places by movements in the ground.

D

DOLOMITE

Type: Sedimentary rock
Colour: White to light brown
Hardness: 3.5–4

Like chalk and limestone, dolomite is made from crushed seashells. As the rock was forming, it was soaked with water full of magnesium. The magnesium made dolomite much stronger than chalk and limestone. Dolomite is often left standing when the rocks around it have worn away.

DYSCRASITE

Type: Mineral

Colour: Silvery grey

Hardness: 3.5–4

This mineral grows in rainwater that soaked into the ground and was then heated by magma. Dyscrasite contains the metal silver, so it is sometimes mined.

EARTHQUAKES

The Earth's crust is split into giant plates of rock, called tectonic plates. When these plates move against each other, it can make the ground shake. This shaking is called an earthquake.

Moving Plates

The Earth's tectonic plates fit together like a jigsaw puzzle. The plates are always moving, and move about 2.5 centimetres each year. Sometimes the plates get caught on each other and shudder. This shuddering quickly travels up through the ground until it is felt at the surface as an earthquake. Most earthquakes happen along the edges of plates.

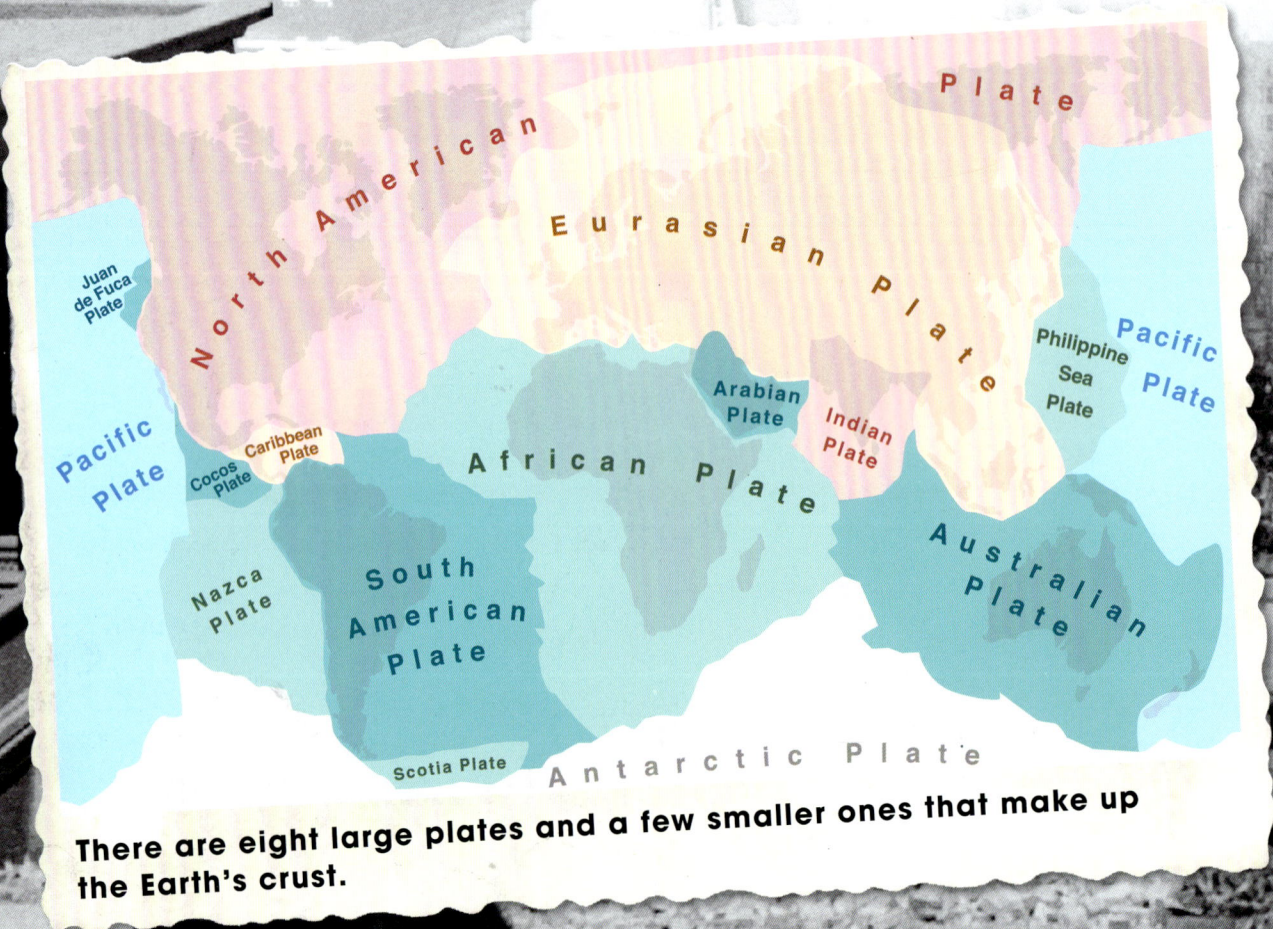

North American Plate

Eurasian Plate

Juan de Fuca Plate

Pacific Plate

Caribbean Plate

Cocos Plate

Arabian Plate

Indian Plate

Philippine Sea Plate

Pacific Plate

African Plate

Nazca Plate

South American Plate

Australian Plate

Scotia Plate

Antarctic Plate

There are eight large plates and a few smaller ones that make up the Earth's crust.

In an Earthquake

There are thousands of earthquakes every year, but most of them are too small to do any damage. In a powerful earthquake, the ground can split open and buildings and bridges can crumble. Scientists are always watching for signs that an earthquake may happen, so they can warn people to stay safe.

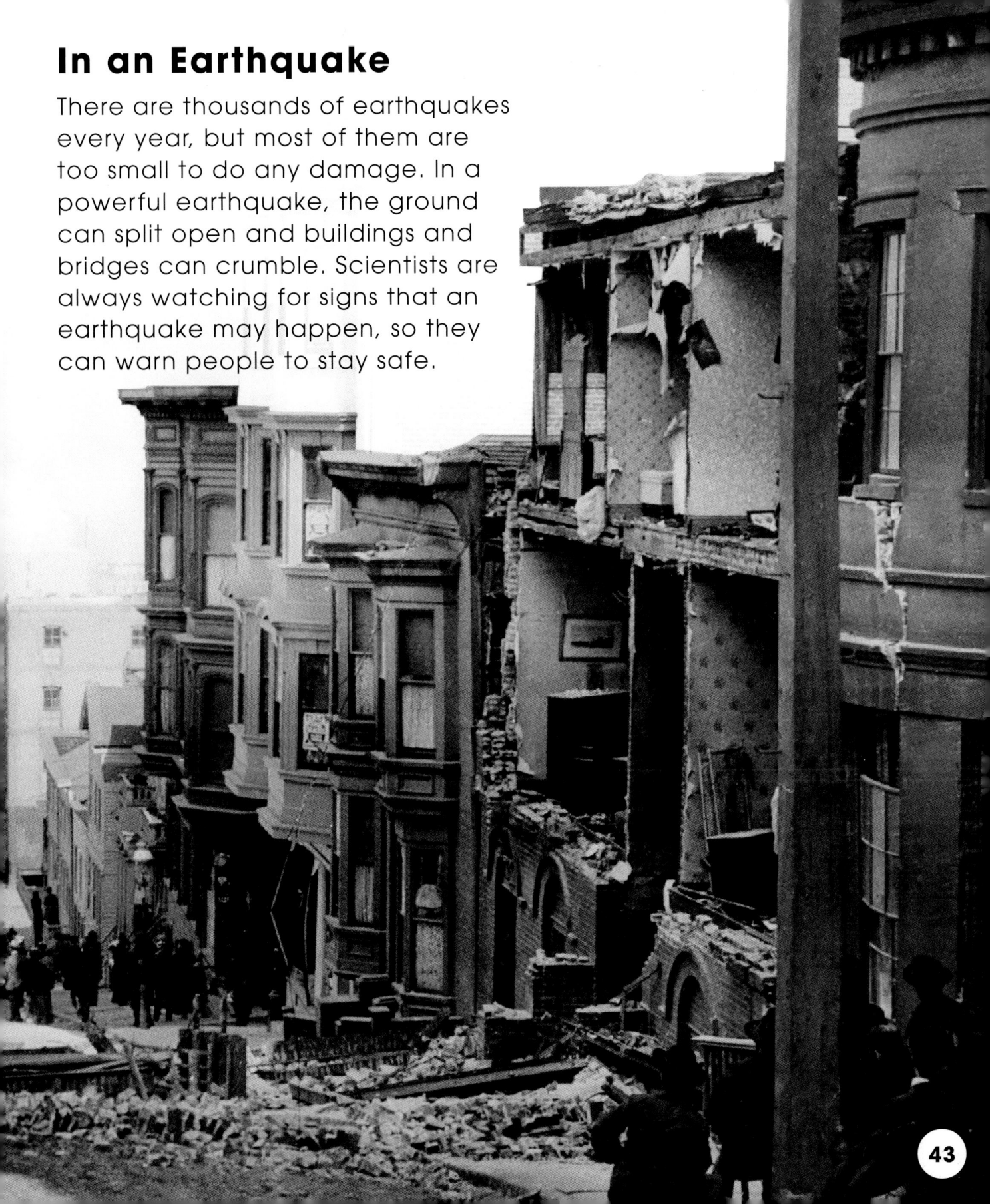

43

E

EPIDOTE

Type: Mineral
Colour: Green
Hardness: 6

Epidote can be found in many shades of green. Its crystals often grow in tall, four-sided blocks. Big crystals can form in metamorphic rocks such as marble.

ERYTHRITE

Type: Mineral

Colour: Pink to red and purple

Hardness: 1.5–2.5

Erythrite is usually found growing as a crust on other minerals. When erythrite does grow large, it forms tall four-sided crystals. In the past, erythrite was used to colour red paint.

FELDSPAR

Type: Mineral

Colour: White, grey, brown, pink or pale blue

Hardness: 6-6.5

Feldspar is a very common mineral that makes up more than half of the Earth's crust. It is part of the mineral mixture that makes rocks like basalt, diorite, gneiss and granite. Pale speckles of feldspar can sometimes be seen in those rocks.

FLINT

Type: Sedimentary rock

Colour: Grey, brown, black, green or white

Hardness: 7

Lumps of hard, glass-like flint are often found in limestone. Flint is made mostly of the mineral quartz. In the Stone Age, flint was used to make arrowheads and tools for cutting.

FLUORITE

Type: Mineral

Colour: Usually colourless, but may be any colour

Hardness: 4

Fluorite is common in igneous and sedimentary rocks. Pure fluorite is colourless and see-through, but this mineral may be any colour if it includes other elements. Pure fluorite can be made into very clear lenses that are used in microscopes and telescopes.

F

FOSSILS

A **fossil** is the hardened remains of an animal or plant that lived millions of years ago. Fossils are often found in rocks. Scientists learned that dinosaurs existed from uncovering their fossils.

Body Fossils

A fossil can be made when a plant or a dead animal is buried by mud or sand. As the mud or sand hardens into rock, the tough parts of the animal or plant also harden. A fossil can show us the shell of a sea creature, the bones of a dinosaur or the stem of a plant.

This is a fossil of a *Keichousaurus*, which lived 247-237 million years ago.

Footprints

If an animal walks across soft mud, it leaves footprints. These footprints can be fossilized if the mud is baked hard by the sun, then covered in more mud or sand.

Dinosaur footprints can tell us how these amazing animals walked.

Amber

The bodies of insects are often found trapped in amber. Millions of years ago, the insect got caught in sticky tree resin, which hardened into amber.

This insect lived millions of years ago.

G

GNEISS

Type: Metamorphic rock

Colour: Stripes of white to gold and grey to black

Hardness: 7

Gneiss can be made when granite is compressed and heated underground by tectonic plates moving towards each other. The compression makes the granite's minerals line up, giving gneiss its striped bands.

GOLD

Type: Metal

Colour: Yellow

Hardness: 2.5-3

Big chunks of gold can be found inside rocks, but little flakes and grains can be washed away into rivers and streams. Gold is valued for its beautiful colour. Gold is mined so it can be melted down and used in jewellery and machinery.

GRANITE

Type: Igneous rock

Colour: White, pink or grey

Hardness: 6-7

Granite is made of magma that cooled slowly deep inside the Earth. When we see granite at the Earth's surface, it has been pushed up by tectonic plate movements and the softer rock above has been worn away. Granite is often speckled with light and dark mineral crystals.

H

HALITE

Type: Mineral

Colour: Usually white or colourless, but may be blue, pink, orange or yellow

Hardness: 2.5

Halite is another name for salt. Halite crystals grow when salty lakes and seas dry up. This mineral is mined, then used to flavour food or to make products like soap.

HORNFELS

Type: Metamorphic rock

Colour: White to green, grey and black

Hardness: 5

Hornfels is made when a rock is baked by super-hot magma. This rock is so tough that ancient people used it to sharpen knives. The hard rock shaved the metal, making a narrow, sharp edge.

HEULANDITE

Type: Mineral

Colour: Colourless, white, yellow, green, pink or red

Hardness: 3–4

This mineral is often found in basalt and other rocks made from hardened lava. Its crystals grow in many different shapes, from clusters of tiny grains to bigger wedges. Heulandite is named after the 19th century mineral collector John Henry Heuland.

IOLITE

Type: Mineral

Colour: Bright blue to violet

Hardness: 7–7.5

This pretty blue mineral is sometimes called a water sapphire, because it is blue but seems to change colour when seen from different angles. Iolite can be found in metamorphic rocks.

IRON

Type: Metal

Colour: Silvery grey

Hardness: 4–5

Iron is one of the most common elements on Earth. It makes up most of the Earth's core and is also common, along with other elements, in the Earth's rocky crust. Iron is a strong metal that is mined so it can be used in construction. When iron is in damp air for a long time, it rusts, which means its surface turns an orangey-brown colour.

J

JADE

Type: Mineral

Colour: Green, red or yellow

Hardness: 6–7

The green gem we call jade can be two different minerals: jadeite or nephrite. Both minerals are found in different colours, but green crystals are coloured by iron or chromium. Jade is often carved and polished to make statues and jewellery.

JASPER

Type: Mineral

Colour: Red, yellow, brown, green, black or blue

Hardness: 6.5–7

Jasper is made mostly of the mineral quartz. It often contains spots or stripes of other minerals, so some people call it a rock rather than a mineral.

J

JEWELLERY

Minerals and rocks can be shaped and polished, then placed in rings, necklaces and earrings. Usually, only the strongest and most beautiful rocks and minerals are chosen for jewellery.

Cabochons

Rocks are usually opaque, which means they cannot be seen through. Opaque rocks and minerals are often cut into a domed shape called a cabochon. They are polished so that their beautiful colours or patterns can be seen clearly.

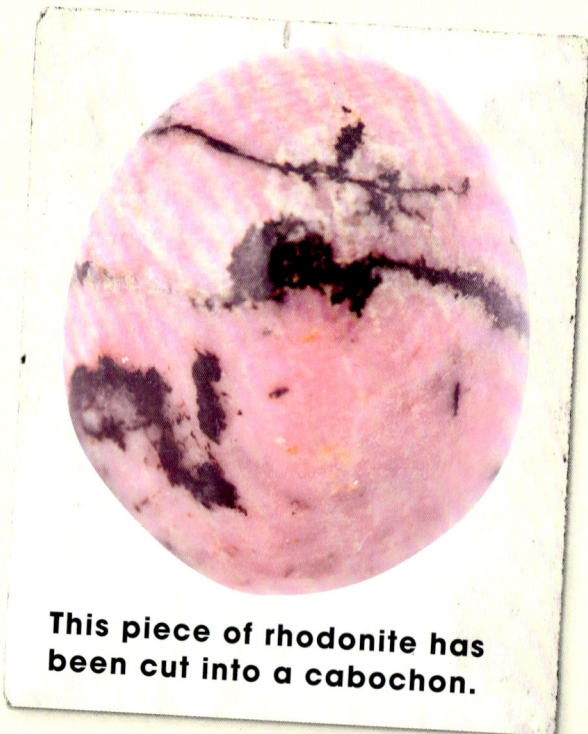

This piece of rhodonite has been cut into a cabochon.

Facets

The most expensive gems are transparent, which means they can be seen through easily. To make them sparkle, they are cut with many straight sides, called facets. The facets bounce light around inside the gem.

Jewellers cut facets using a machine with a rough, spinning wheel.

K

KIMBERLITE

Type: Igneous rock

Colour: Brown to grey

Hardness: 6–7

Diamonds are often found in kimberlite. This rock is made deep inside the Earth. It is named after the town of Kimberley in South Africa, where a large hole, called the Big Hole, was dug into the kimberlite to mine its diamonds.

KUTNOHORITE

Type: Mineral

Colour: White to pale pink

Hardness: 3.5–4

This rare mineral is named after the place it was first found: Kutná Hora in the Czech Republic. Kutnohorite often grows as bundles of blade-shaped crystals.

KYANITE

Type: Mineral

Colour: Blue

Hardness: 4–7

Kyanite is made when sedimentary rocks are compressed by tectonic plates that are moving together. Crystals usually grow as four-sided blocks.

L

LABRADORITE

Type: Mineral

Colour: Grey, brown, green or blue

Hardness: 6–6.5

This mineral is iridescent, which means that it shines in a rainbow of colours when it catches the light. It was first found in Labrador, Canada, where it was dug from igneous rocks.

LAPIS LAZULI

Type: Metamorphic rock

Colour: Blue, with white and gold

Hardness: 5–6

For thousands of years, this beautiful blue rock has been used in jewellery, statues and art. Its name means 'stone of the heavens'. It contains the blue mineral lazurite, as well as the white mineral calcite and the golden mineral pyrite.

L

LIMESTONE

Type: Sedimentary rock

Colour: White and cream to grey

Hardness: 3-4

This pale-coloured rock is made mostly of crushed shells that piled up on the seafloor. Many of the fossils discovered by scientists have been found in limestone. Limestone is also easily dissolved by rainwater, which means that small bits of limestone are carried away by the water. Over many years, limestone washed by rainwater is shaped into peaks and caves.

M

MALACHITE

Type: Mineral

Colour: Green

Hardness: 3.5–4

Malachite forms in holes and cracks in rock. It often grows in layers, giving it stripes. Malachite is sometimes carved into vases and statues.

MARBLE

Type: Metamorphic rock

Colour: White, but may be streaked pink, green, blue or black

Hardness: 3–4

If limestone is crushed between tectonic plates, it becomes white marble. When the limestone contains bits of sand, clay or iron, these create coloured swirls in the marble. Marble is strong but easy to cut, so it has often been used to construct great buildings, such as India's Taj Mahal.

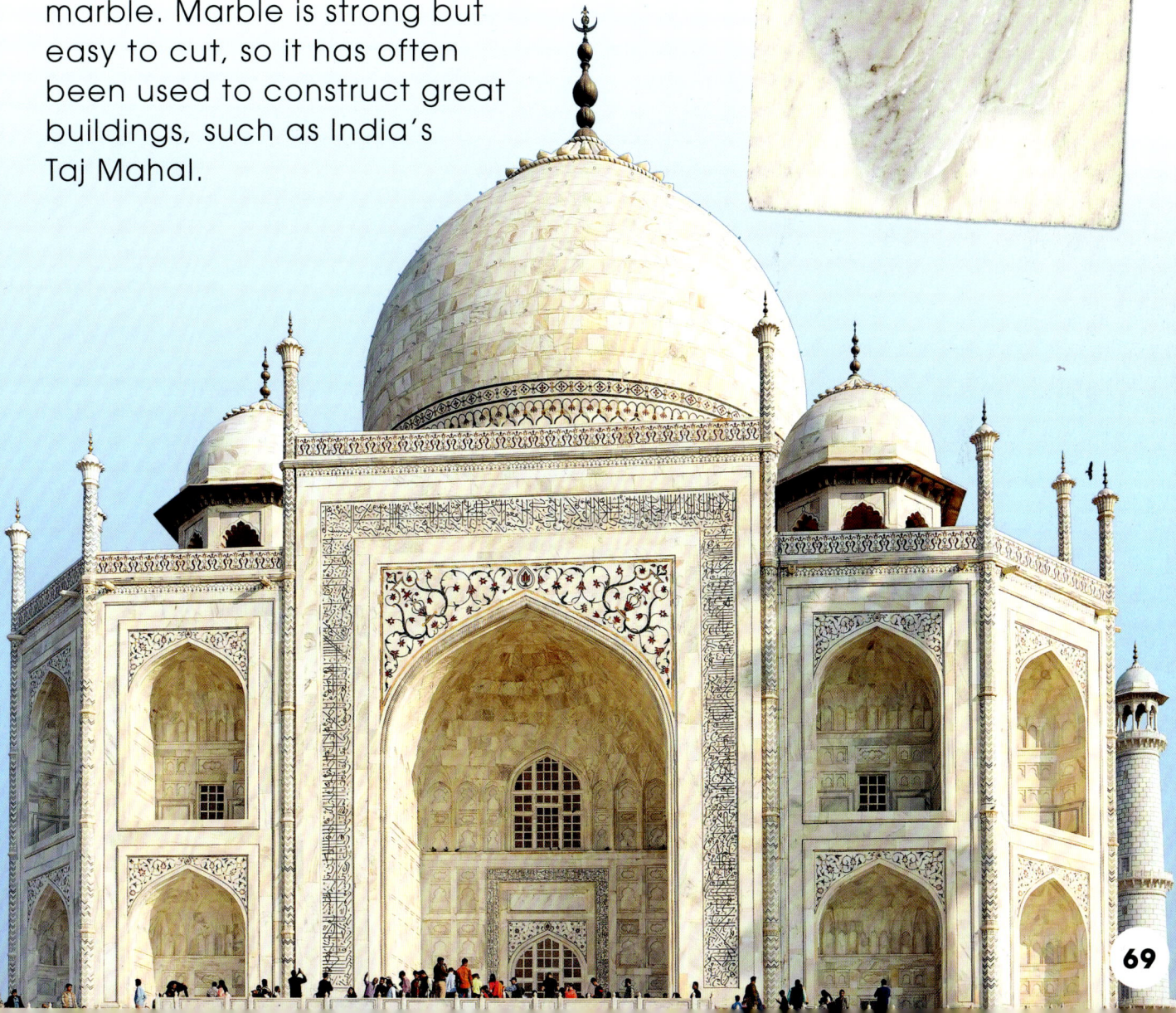

M

MOUNTAINS

Mountains are made by the Earth's tectonic plates moving towards each other. Very slowly, the movement folds or cracks the rock to form mountains. Most mountains are part of mountain ranges, where lots of mountains are found together in a line.

Folding

The world's tallest mountain is Mount Everest, which is 8848 metres high. It is part of the Himalayan mountain range in Asia. These mountains started to form about 50 million years ago as one tectonic plate slid under another. This folded the rock, pushing it up like crumpled paper.

Moving tectonic plates are causing Mount Everest to grow about 0.5 centimetres taller each year.

Cracking

Moving plates can sometimes crack the rock. Some of the broken pieces are pushed up, while others sink down.

The Wasatch mountain range in Utah, United States, is made of broken blocks of rock.

M

MUDSTONE

Type: Sedimentary rock

Colour: Black, brown, grey or white

Hardness: 2–3

This rock is made from mud that has been pressed hard beneath layers of clay, mud or sand. Mud is a mixture of water and small bits of minerals. As mudstone is formed, the water is squeezed out, leaving the minerals stuck to each other.

N

NAGYÁGITE

Type: Mineral

Colour: Dark grey to black

Hardness: 1–1.5

This mineral, which often grows near gold, was first found in the Nagyág gold mine in Romania. It contains gold, as well as lead and sulphur.

NATROLITE

Type: Mineral

Colour: Usually white or colourless

Hardness: 5–5.5

Natrolite is also known as needle stone, because it often grows in long, thin needles, forming tufts like grass. This mineral can be found inside holes in igneous rocks.

NEPTUNITE

Type: Mineral

Colour: Black

Hardness: 5–6

Neptunite was named after Neptune, the Roman god of the sea, because it can be found close to the mineral aegirine, named after Aegir, the Scandinavian sea god. Neptunite crystals grow in four-sided blocks.

OBSIDIAN

Type: Igneous rock

Colour: Black

Hardness: 5–5.5

This rock is made when thick lava cools down quickly. It cools so fast that its mineral crystals do not have time to grow. These tiny crystals make obsidian smooth like glass. When obsidian is broken, it is left with sharp edges. Thousands of years ago, humans used obsidian for tools and weapons.

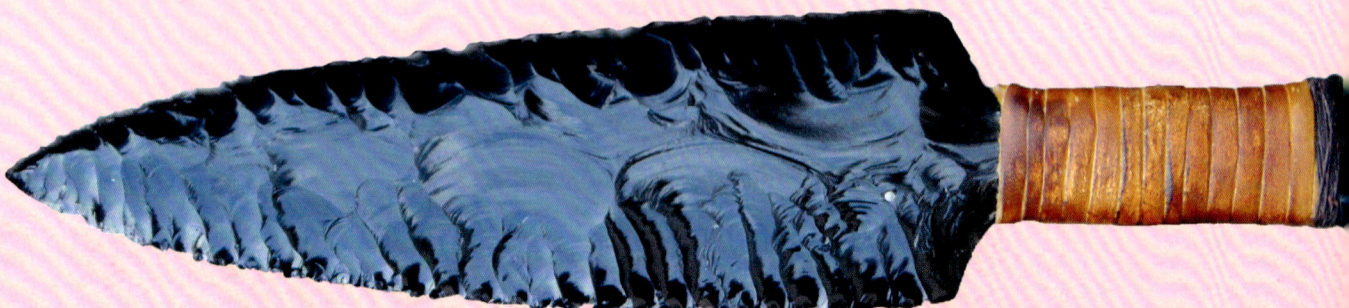

OÖLITE

Type: Sedimentary rock

Colour: Usually white or cream

Hardness: 3-4

Oölite means 'egg stone'. It starts to form when a piece of shell or sand rolls around in water that is full of minerals. Some of the minerals stick to the shell or sand, making it grow larger until it joins together with other 'eggs' to form solid rock.

ORES

An ore is a rock or mineral that contains lots of metal or another valuable mineral. Metals have many different uses, in things from phones to skyscrapers. To get these useful metals, ores are dug from the ground in mines.

Useful Mixes

Around 90 metals can be found in the ground, most of which are dug up with other elements. Only a few metals, like gold and silver, are found in solid, pure chunks. Most of the metals we use are taken from ores. Once the ore has been mined, it is heated to break it up and separate the metals.

Ores are heated up to remove the metals or minerals in them.

Jobs for Metals

Bright-coloured metals are often used in jewellery and mirrors. Because metals are strong but easy to bend, they can be shaped into beams for constructing houses, into knives, or made into parts for cars. Some metals allow heat and electricity to travel through them easily, so they are used for electrical wires or for cooking equipment.

Aluminum is a strong, lightweight metal, so it is used for making cars.

P

PERIDOT

Type: Mineral

Colour: Olive green

Hardness: 6.5–7

Peridot is the name given to the mineral olivine when it is olive green and see-through. Peridot is used as a gemstone. Olivine, which can also be yellow, is found in many igneous rocks.

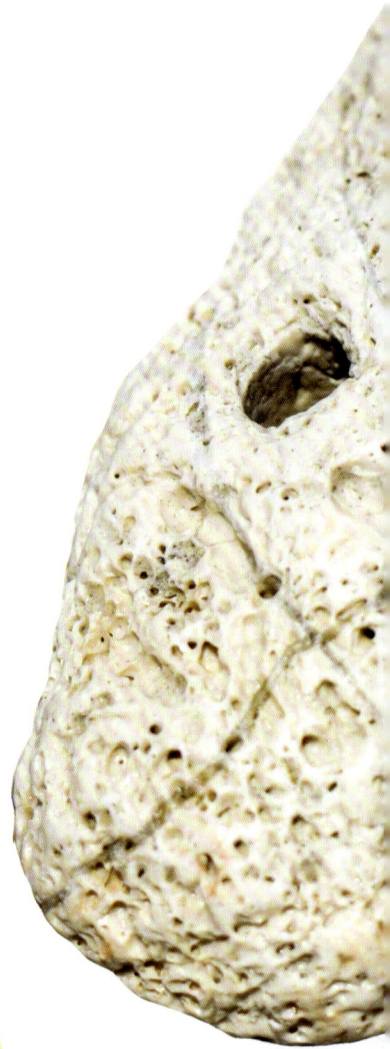

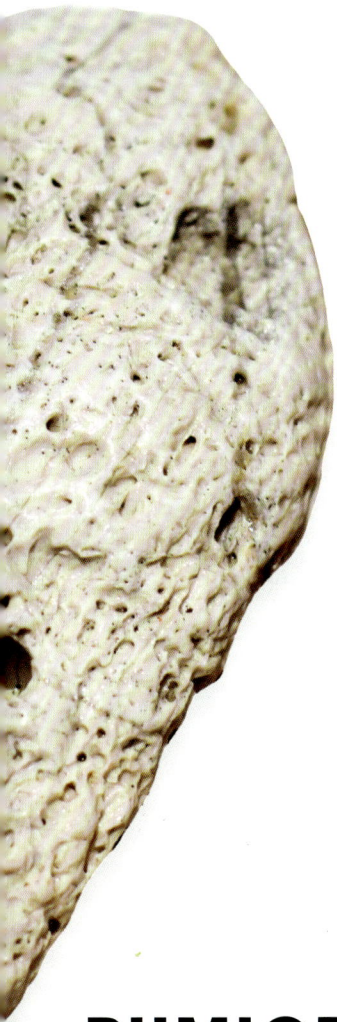

PYRITE

Type: Mineral

Colour: Pale yellow

Hardness: 6–6.5

This mineral is often called fool's gold, because its colour is so similar to the yellow of gold. Pyrite grows in cube-shaped crystals. In its purest form, this mineral contains only two elements: iron and sulphur.

PUMICE

Type: Igneous rock

Colour: White to pale brown

Hardness: 6

Pumice forms when lava is thrown from a volcano in a fierce eruption. The lava is full of gas bubbles and cools very quickly, leaving pumice with many holes. This rock is lightweight and rough to touch.

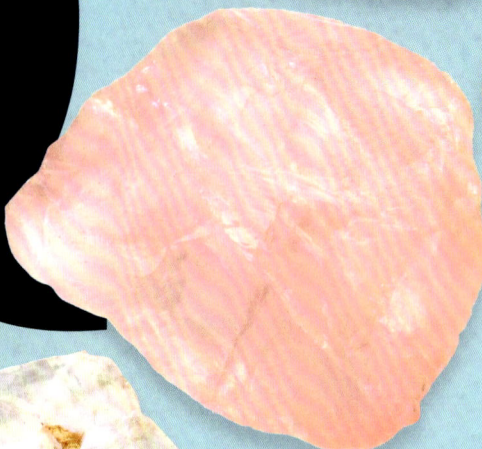

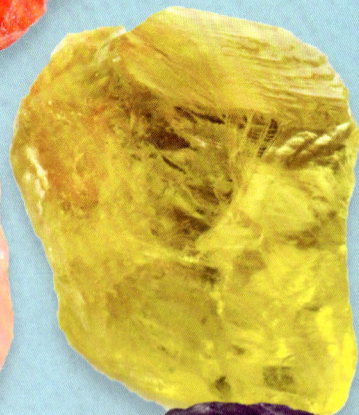

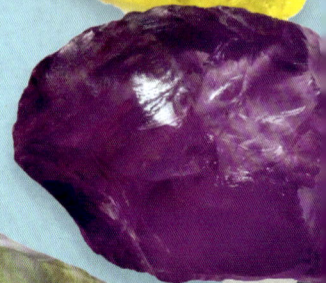

QUARTZ

Type: Mineral

Colour: Colourless, but may be tinted any colour

Hardness: 7

Quartz is made of silicon and oxygen. Pure quartz is see-through and colourless, but it can be tinted many colours. When quartz is purple, it is known as amethyst, which is a beautiful and expensive gem. Yellow quartz is known as citrine, while carnelian is red quartz.

QUARTZITE

Type: Metamorphic rock

Colour: Usually cream to grey, but may be tinted pink or red

Hardness: 6-7

This rock is made from sandstone that has lots of quartz crystals. As the sandstone is pressed by tectonic plates, the quartz crystals are fixed tight to each other. This makes quartzite a very strong rock.

R

RHYOLITE

Type: Igneous rock
Colour: Pink or grey
Hardness: 6–7

This rock is made of super-thick, cooled lava. Not many volcanoes erupt the kind of lava that makes rhyolite, so it is not a very common rock. Gold and gems such as agate, beryl and opal are sometimes found in holes and cracks in rhyolite.

R

ROSELITE

Type: Mineral

Colour: Red to pink

Hardness: 3.5

Surprisingly, roselite was not named for its rose-like colour – it was named for the 19th century mineral collector Gustave Rose. If roselite crystals have room to grow, they form tall, four-sided blocks, but they are more commonly found as small crystals coating cracks in rock.

RUBY

Type: Mineral

Colour: Red

Hardness: 9

When the mineral corundum is transparent and red, it is called ruby. Since they are so beautiful and their colour is so striking, rubies are very expensive gemstones. Corundum is made in the great heat when igneous and metamorphic rocks form.

RUTILE

Type: Mineral

Colour: Red-brown, yellow, blue, green, violet or black

Hardness: 6–6.5

Although some rutile crystals grow alone inside rocks, this mineral often grows inside other minerals. Rutile crystals form as needles inside quartz, rubies and sapphires.

S

SAND

Sand is small pieces of rocks and minerals. It can be any colour, depending on its composition. Sand is found on beaches, in deserts and beside rivers.

Making Sand

Sand is made when rock is broken up by wind or water. On beaches, sand may also contain broken bits of shells and corals. Sand forms where rock is not covered by mud and plants, most commonly in deserts, oceans and along cliffs.

In a desert, sand can be whipped up into a terrifying sandstorm.

Moving Sand

Once sand is made, it is easily carried along by wind or water. In deserts, the wind can pile it up, creating tall dunes. By the sea, sand can be carried along the coast by waves, sometimes forming long ridges called spits.

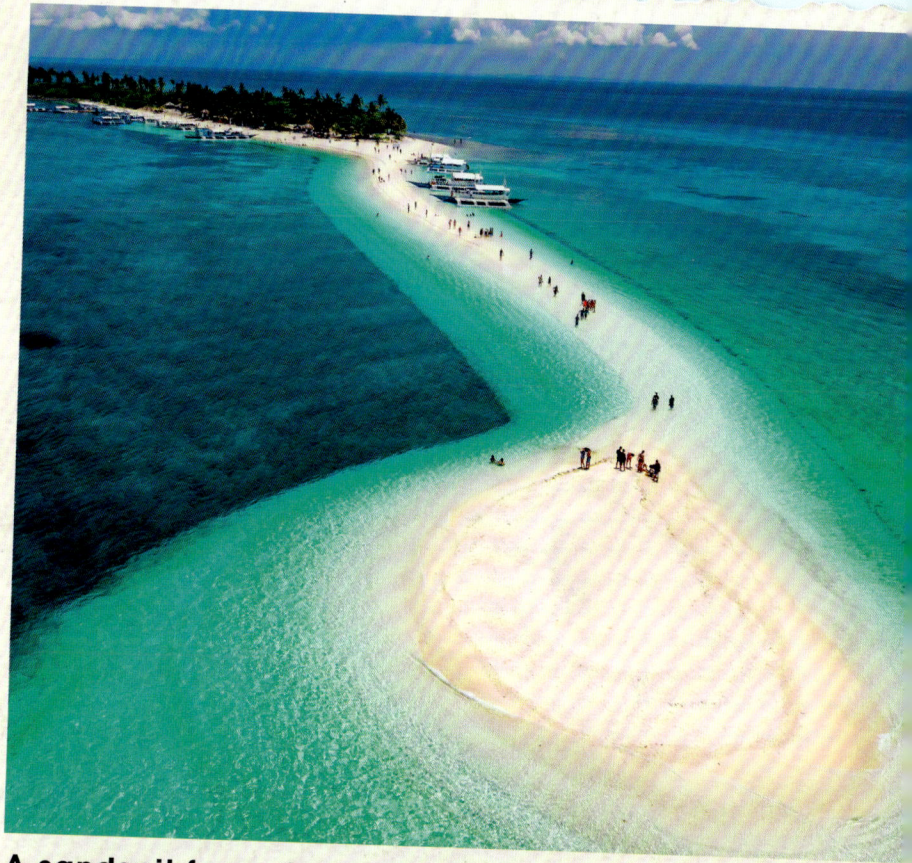

A sandspit forms in shallow water.

S

SANDSTONE

Type: Sedimentary rock

Colour: Yellow, pink, red, brown, grey or black

Hardness: 6–7

Sandstone is made from sand. When sand piles up at the bottom of a sea or river, the grains are slowly – over thousands of years – pressed tightly together until they harden. Uluru in Australia is a huge block of sandstone.

S

SILVER

Type: Metal

Colour: Pale grey

Hardness: 2.5-3

This shiny metal can be found in rocks, on its own or mixed with other minerals. Silver is used in jewellery, mirrors, electrical products and medical tools.

SLATE

Type: Metamorphic rock

Colour: Dark grey

Hardness: 3-4

When mudstones are pressed between tectonic plates, they can turn into slate. In this rock, the mineral crystals are lined up in layers, which means that slate is easily split into flat sheets.

SOAPSTONE

Type: Metamorphic rock

Colour: Grey to brown

Hardness: 1

This rock contains the soft mineral talc. It is so soft it is easy to carve into statues, ornaments and utensils. Soapstone is formed when underground rocks that contain large amounts of talc are heated and compressed.

TANZANITE

Type: Mineral

Colour: Blue to violet

Hardness: 6.5–7

Tanzanite is found only in Tanzania, Africa. Large crystals are usually tall, four-sided blocks. They seem to change from blue to violet to dark purple when looked at from different angles.

TIGER'S EYE

Type: Metamorphic rock

Colour: Gold to red-brown

Hardness: 7

This rock is named for the vertical band that shines like a cat's eye. This effect is caused by the way the rock's quartz and other mineral crystals are arranged side by side. Tiger's eye can be polished, cut and worn in jewellery.

TOPAZ

Type: Mineral

Colour: Colourless, but may be tinted green, red, orange and pink

Hardness: 8

When pure, this mineral is clear and colourless, but impurities can tint it many pretty shades. Topaz is very hard, so it is often used in jewellery and carvings.

T

TUFF

Type: Igneous rock

Colour: Cream to grey

Hardness: 4-6

Tuff forms when **ash** is thrown out of a volcano. After the ash settles and cools, it slowly hardens into this soft rock. In Turkey, spires of tuff were carved into homes.

U

UNAKITE

Type: Metamorphic rock
Colour: Green and pink
Hardness: 6–7

This colourful rock is carved into jewellery, statues and floor tiles. It started out as granite, which was heated and compressed until pink crystals of orthoclase and green epidote formed.

UVAROVITE

Type: Mineral

Colour: Green

Hardness: 7–7.5

Uvarovite is usually found as very small green crystals. If given the time and space to grow, uvarovite crystals can form large cubes or 12-sided shapes. This mineral contains chromium, which gives its bright-green colour, as well as calcium, silicon and oxygen.

V

VANADINITE

Type: Mineral

Colour: Usually red

Hardness: 2.5–3

This mineral grows as six-sided crystals. It contains vanadium, lead, chlorine and oxygen. Vanadinite is mined, then heated to remove the vanadium and lead, which are useful metals.

VESUVIANITE

Type: Mineral

Colour: Green, brown, yellow or blue

Hardness: 6.5

Vesuvianite was first found on Mount Vesuvius, a volcano in Italy. This mineral grows in rocks like limestone when they are heated by lava.

VAUXITE

Type: Mineral

Colour: Blue

Hardness: 3.5

Vauxite was named after American mineral collector George Vaux. Often small, vauxite crystals grow side by side in rock crevices. This mineral is found only in Bolivia, in South America, and in Pennsylvania.

V

VOLCANOES

Volcanoes are holes or cracks in the Earth's crust where melted rock escapes. Many volcanoes are shaped like mountains. This shape is made by many layers of cooled, hardened lava.

Where Are Volcanoes?

Most volcanoes are near the edges of tectonic plates. This is because when rock is squeezed between moving plates, it can melt into magma and rise to the surface. A few volcanoes are in the middle of tectonic plates, over unusually hot spots in the mantle. These are called hotspot volcanoes.

Stromboli has small but explosive eruptions.

Eruption

Beneath a volcano is a pool of melted rock, called a magma chamber. When large amounts of magma pour into the chamber, or the chamber gets really hot and gassy, the volcano will erupt. In an eruption, lava, rocks, ash and gas can all spill from a volcano. Some eruptions are fast and explosive, while others are slow and steady.

Active or Not?

When a volcano erupts quite regularly, it is called an active volcano. When a volcano no longer has a magma chamber underneath it, it is an extinct volcano that will never erupt again. Some volcanoes still have magma in their chambers but have not erupted in thousands of years. These are called dormant volcanoes.

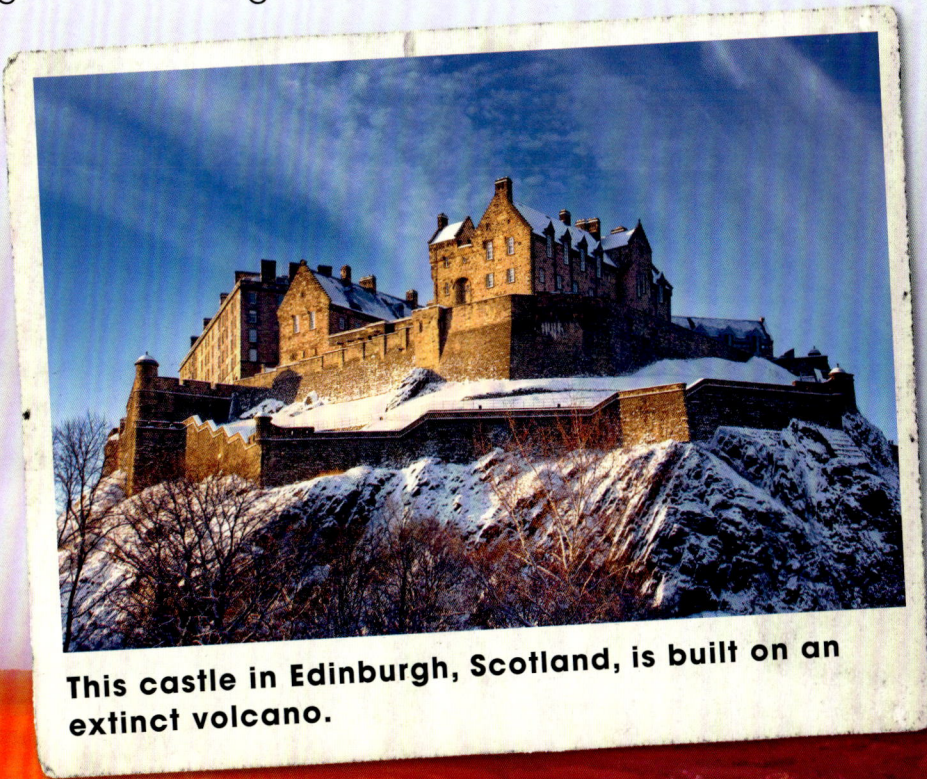

This castle in Edinburgh, Scotland, is built on an extinct volcano.

W

WACKESTONE

Type: Sedimentary rock

Colour: Cream

Hardness: 6–7

Wackestone is made of crushed seashells, mud and sand. This makes the rock look and feel both like limestone and mudstone. Wackestone is used for sculptures because it is easy to carve.

WARDITE

Type: Mineral

Colour: Colourless, white, yellow, pink, pale blue or pale green

Hardness: 4.5–5

This rare mineral often grows in pyramid-shaped blocks. It is usually pale-coloured and can be seen through. Wardite was named after the 19th century American mineral collector Henry Augustus Ward, who found it among igneous rocks.

W

WATERFALLS

A waterfall is where a river or stream flows over the edge of a cliff. Waterfalls form where a river has worn away the rock beneath it. People travel from all over the world to see high, beautiful waterfalls.

Making a Waterfall

As rivers rush along, carrying rocks and pebbles, they wear away the rock in the riverbed. A river can wear away soft rock much more quickly than it wears away hard rock. A waterfall can form where the riverbed changes from hard rock to soft rock.

Making a Pool

At the bottom of a waterfall, a bowl-shaped pool starts to grow. This is called a plunge pool. As the water falls onto the rock below, over time it creates a bigger and bigger pool.

Angel Falls in Venezuela is the world's tallest waterfall at 979 metres high.

The 2.7-kilometre-wide Iguazu Falls in South America has formed a huge plunge pool.

W

WAVELLITE

Type: Mineral

Colour: Usually green

Hardness: 3.5–4

Wavellite grows in circles, with its tiny green crystals all pointing towards the centre of the circle. This mineral was first discovered by English physician William Wavell in 1805.

WULFENITE

Type: Mineral

Colour: Orange to red

Hardness: 3

Crystals of wulfenite are usually flat, square plates. In lead mines, minerals containing lead slowly change into wulfenite after being in contact with oxygen in the air. Because of this process, wulfenite contains lead, oxygen and molybdenum.

X

XENOLITH

Type: Any rock within an igneous rock

Colour: Depends on the rock type

Hardness: Varies depending on the original rock

The word 'xenolith' comes from the ancient Greek word '*xeno*', meaning strange, and the Latin word '*lith*', meaning stone. A xenolith is a chunk of rock that is dragged along by flowing magma or lava. When the magma cools into rock, the other chunk of rock becomes stuck inside it.

XENOTIME

Type: Mineral

Colour: Brown, grey or yellow

Hardness: 4.5

This mineral is usually opaque. It is found in igneous rocks. Xenotime has been known to be slightly radioactive, which means it gives off energy that could be harmful to humans in large quantities.

Y

YOGO SAPPHIRE

Type: Mineral

Colour: Blue

Hardness: 9

When the mineral corundum is any colour but red, it is called sapphire. A red corundum is a ruby. The pretty sapphires mined from Yogo, Montana, in the United States, are always blue. Corundum is made of aluminum and oxygen. Small amounts of iron and titanium turn it blue.

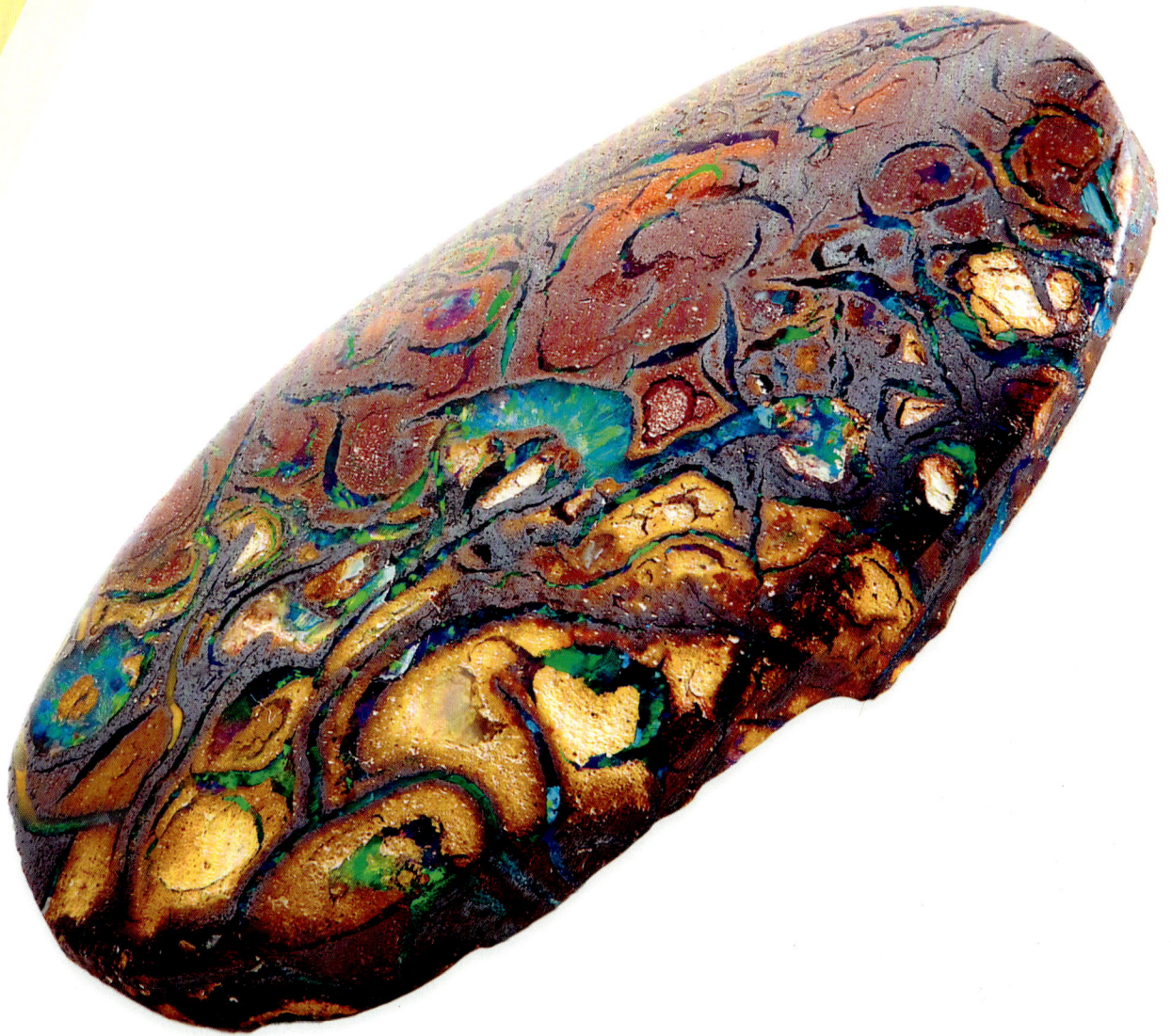

YOWAH NUT OPAL

Type: Mineraloid

Colour: White or any colour of the rainbow

Hardness: 5.5–6.5

An opal is a mineraloid, which is a solid that looks like a mineral but does not have the regular structure of a mineral. An opal shines like a rainbow as it breaks up light into all its colours. Opals from Yowah, Australia, are called yowah nuts. These small rocks can be cracked open like a nut to reveal the opal inside.

Z

ZEBRA STONE

Type: Sedimentary rock

Colour: White and red-brown

Hardness: 7

This rock has layers of pale quartz and dark mudstone, giving it stripes a little like a zebra's. It is found only in western Australia and is used for carvings and jewellery. The patterns may have been created when muddy water flowed through the rock while it was forming.

ZIRCON

Type: Mineral
Colour: Colourless, yellow, green, red or blue
Hardness: 6.5–7.5

Colourless, clear zircons are sometimes used in jewellery because they look like diamonds, but are less hard and therefore much less expensive. Zircons grow in igneous and metamorphic rocks around the world as they are cooling.

ZINKENITE

Type: Mineral
Colour: Grey
Hardness: 3–3.5

This shiny mineral contains the metal lead. Zinkenite usually forms clusters of needle-like crystals. It was discovered in 1824 by German mineral collector Johann Zinken.

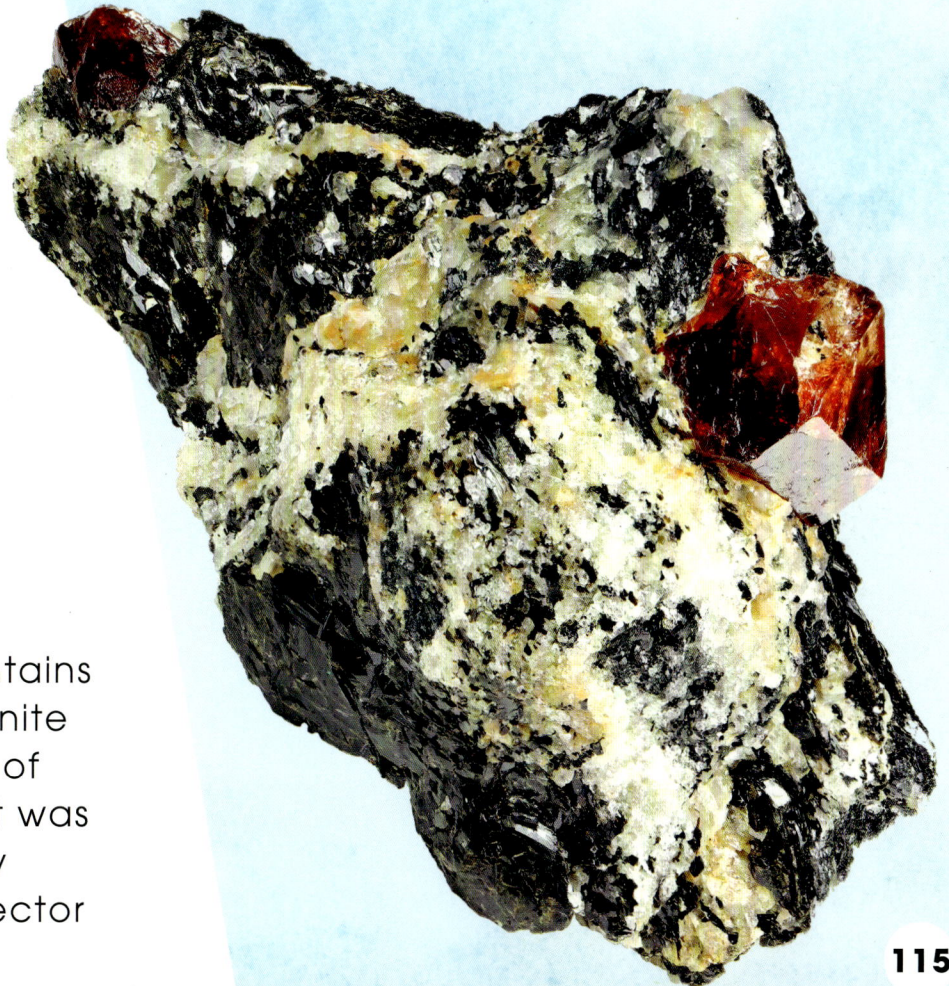

A

B

C

G
H

I

M
N

O

S
T

U

V

D E F

J K L

P Q R

W X Y Z

GLOSSARY

Ash: small pieces of rocks and minerals

Atmosphere: the air surrounding Earth

Atoms: the smallest parts of an element that can exist alone

Compressed: pressed together or flattened by great force

Crystal: a mineral that has formed a regular shape

Element: one of 118 simple materials that are the building blocks for everything on Earth

Erosion: the wearing away of rock by weather, water, or ice

Evaporate: to change from a liquid to a gas

Fertilizer: a material that is added to soil to help plants to grow

Fossil: the hardened remains of an animal or plant that died millions of years ago

Gemstones: a mineral or rock that is so beautiful and hard that people will pay lots of money to own it

Geologists: scientists who study the Earth and its rocks

Metal: a solid that is shiny and can be bent. Pure metals are elements that can be found inside the Earth

Minerals: solids made when atoms of one or more elements join together in a regular pattern

Rock: a solid that is a mixture of minerals

Sediment: small bits of rock, mineral, plants or dead animals

Stalactites: columns of rocks or minerals that hang from the roof of a cave in the shape of icicles

Picture Credits

t = top, b = bottom, l = left, r = right, c = centre